LETTER TRACING FOR KIDS

DELANEY

TRACE MY NAME WORKBOOK

Can't Find Your Name?

Have our elves create a personalized book with the name of your choice today!

VISIT US AT:

PersonalizeThisBook.com

Chiquita publishing

Cover and page design by Cool Journals Studios - Copyright 2017

ABOUT ME

MY NAME IS:

Delaney

I AM ☐ **YEARS OLD.**

I LIVE IN:

For parents

For kids

DRAW YOU AND YOUR FAMILY

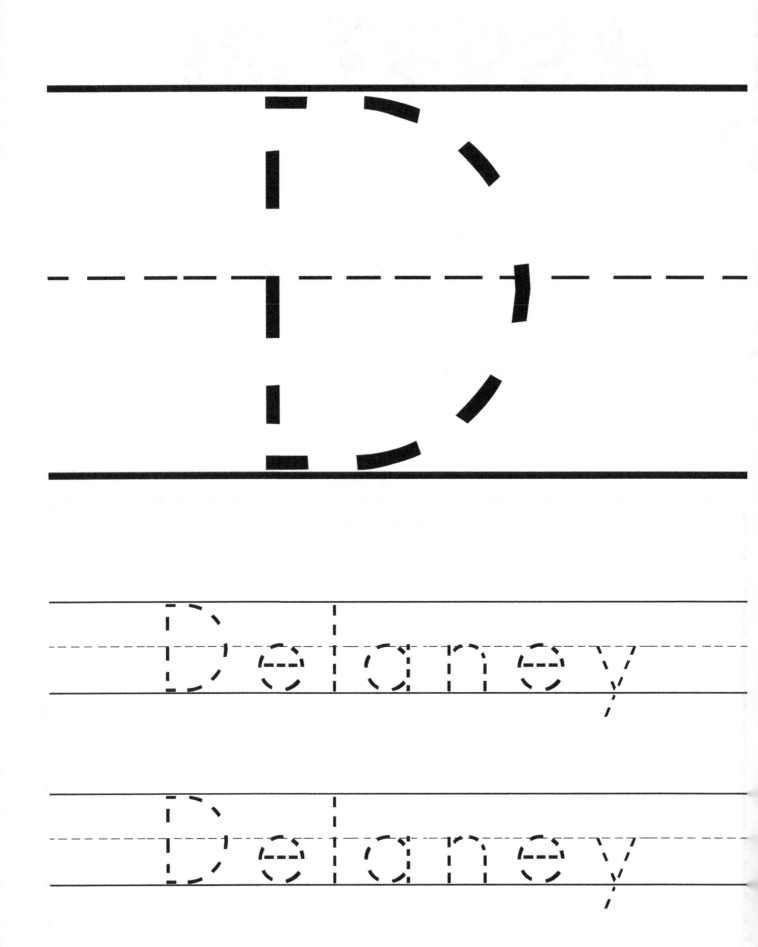

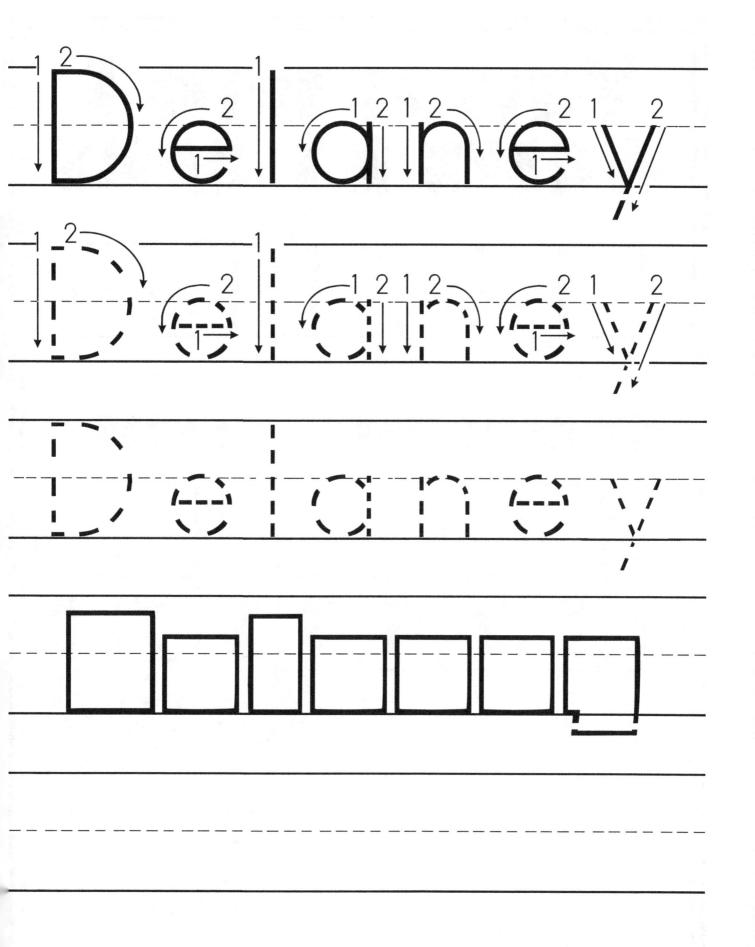

THIS IS HOW I WRITE MY NAME

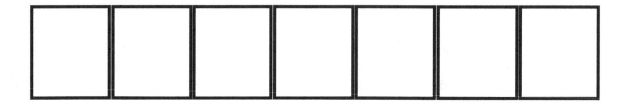

MY NAME HAS ____ LETTERS

1	2	3	4	5	6	7	8

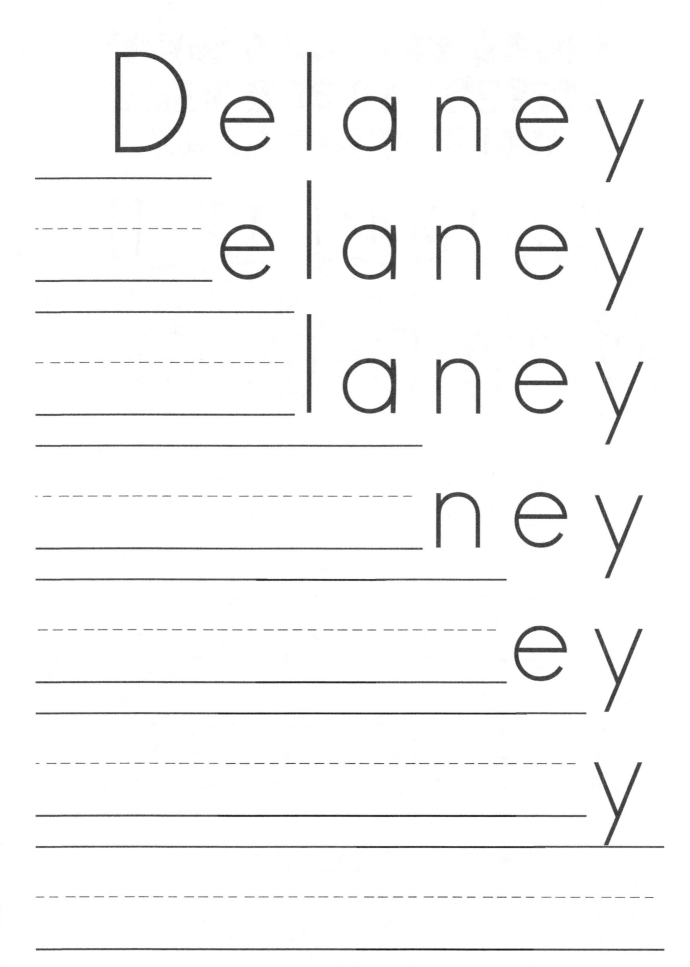

COLOR THE EGGS WITH LETTERS OF OUR NAME WRITE YOUR NAME

P B M F I
V T D E S
Z N L C J
R A Y Q W
G U K O H
E

WRITE YOUR NAME

Delaney

WRITE YOU NAME WITH.

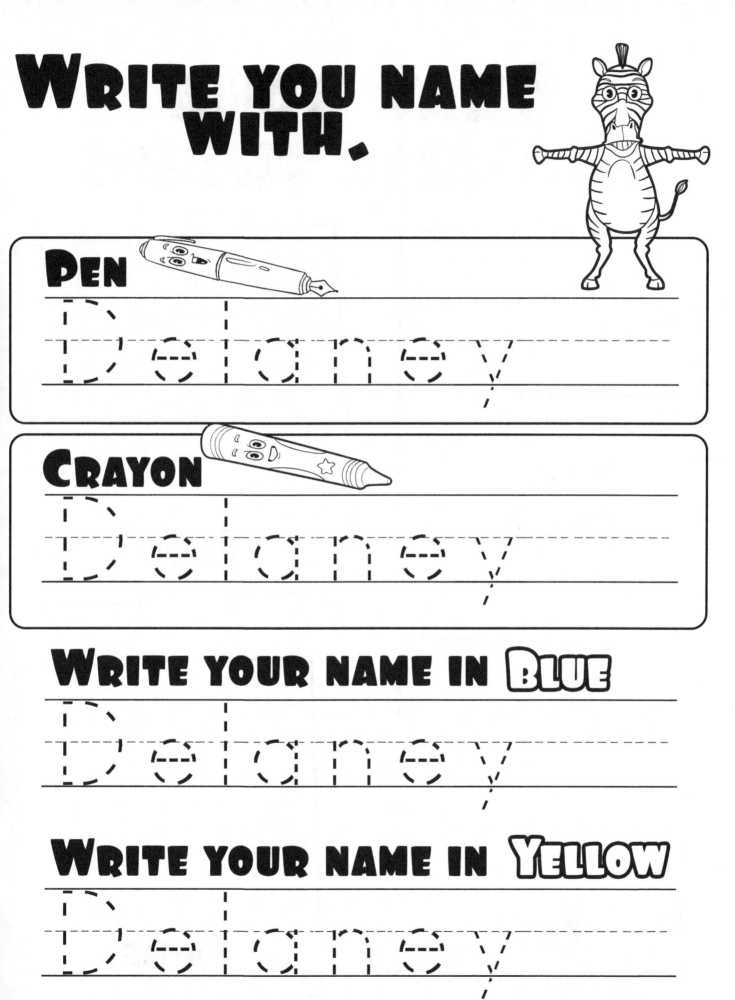

PEN

Delaney

CRAYON

Delaney

WRITE YOUR NAME IN BLUE

Delaney

WRITE YOUR NAME IN YELLOW

Delaney

DRAW YOUR FAVORITE THINGS

COLOR

FOOD

TOY

ANIMAL

MY NAME

My name STARTS WITH	My name ENDS WITH
_____	_____

FILL THE LETTERS OF YOUR NAME WHITH DIFFERENT COLORS

P B W F V I T

D E S Z N L C

J R A Y Q K

G U E O H M

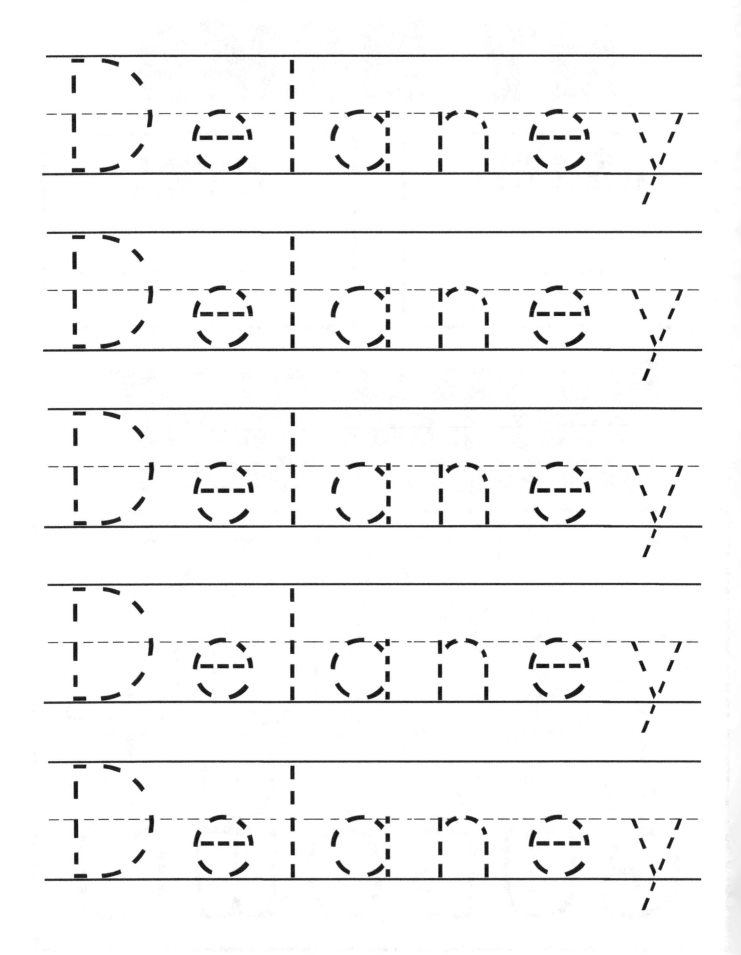

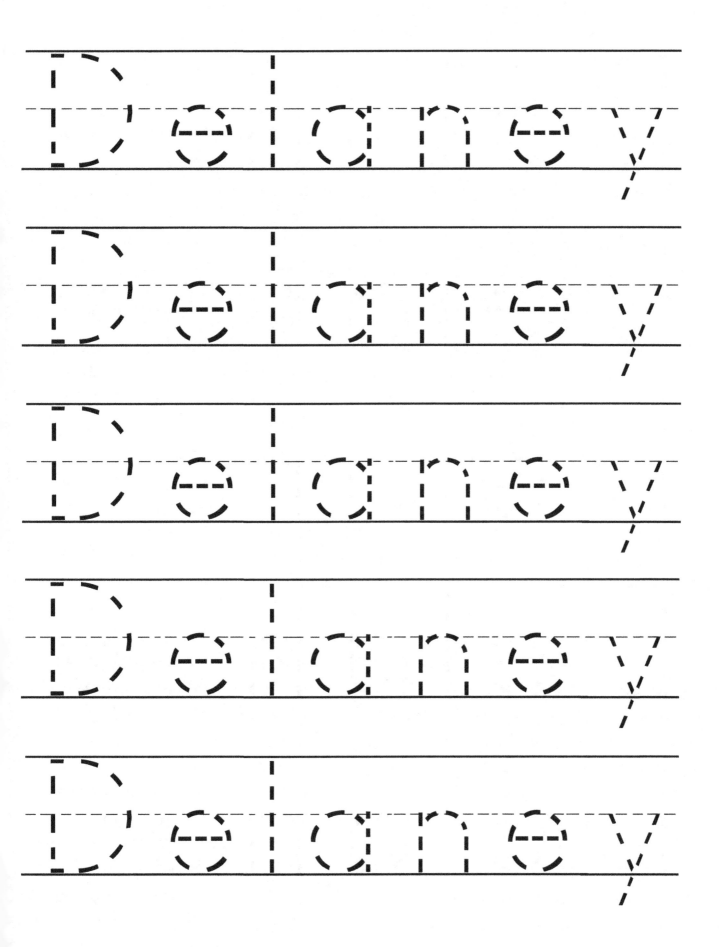

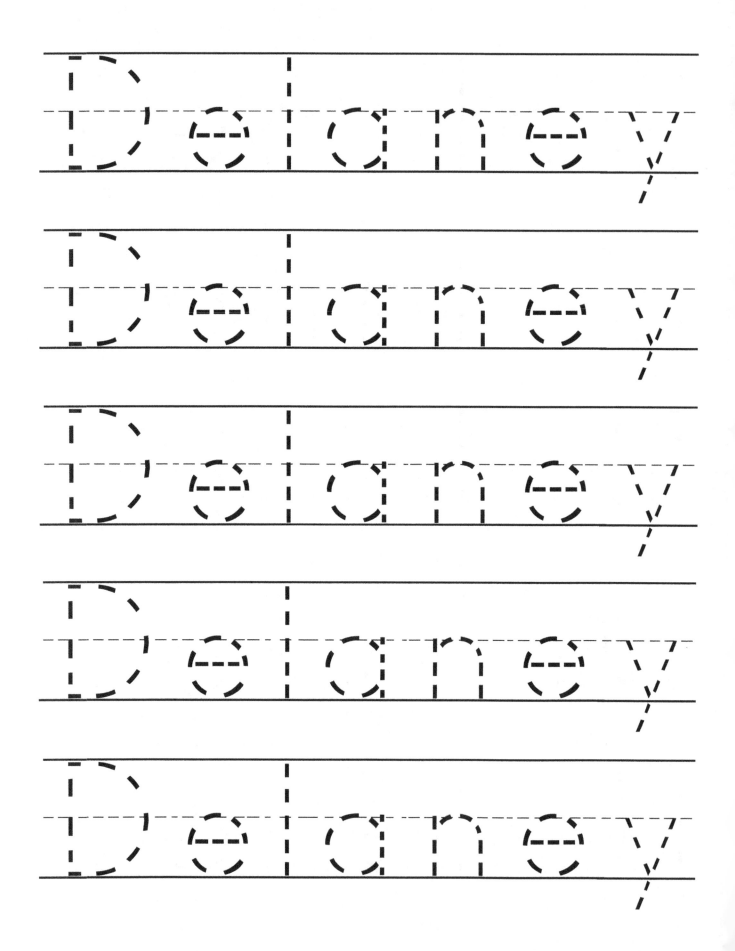

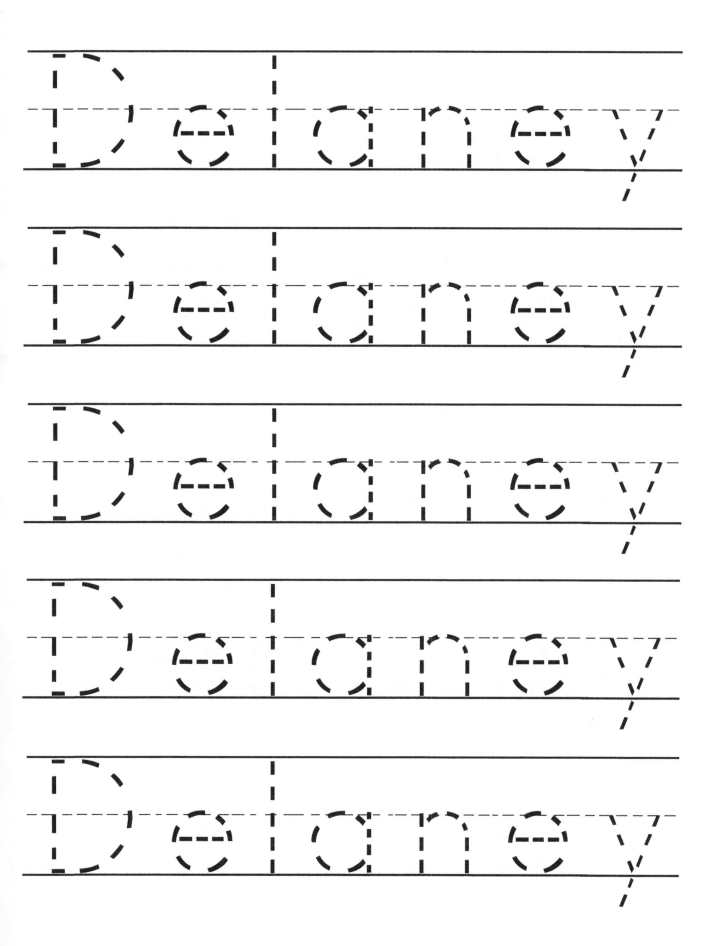

Delaney

Delaney

Delaney

Delaney

Delaney

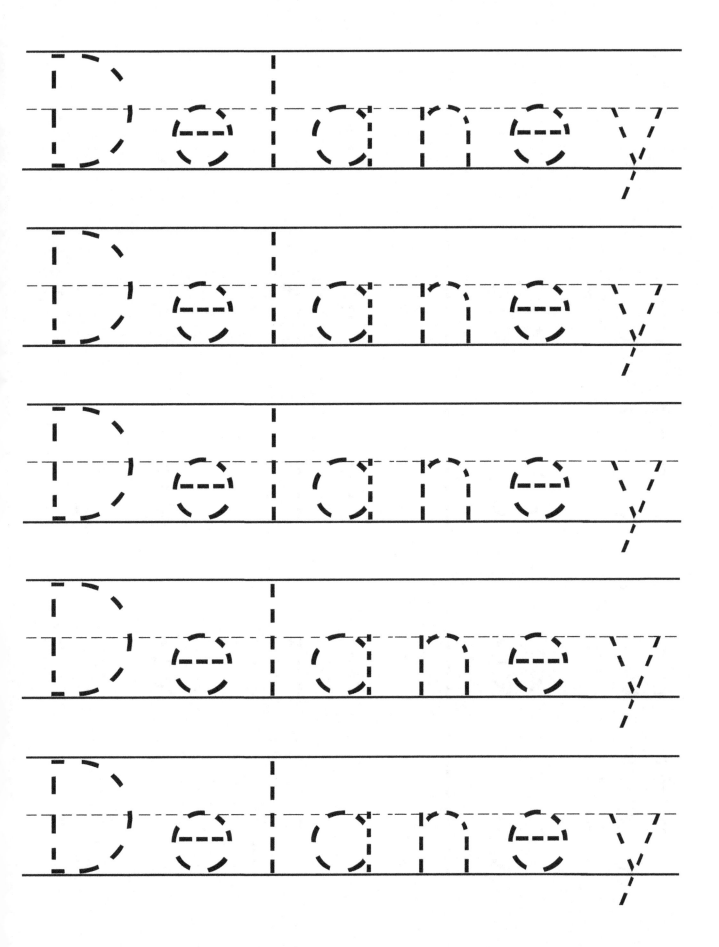

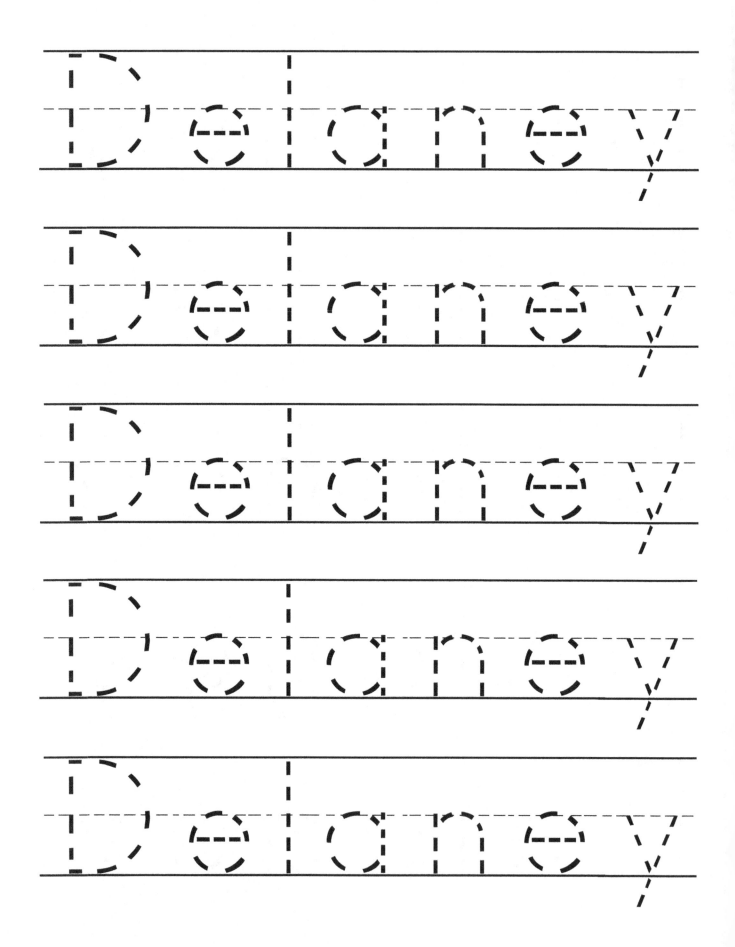

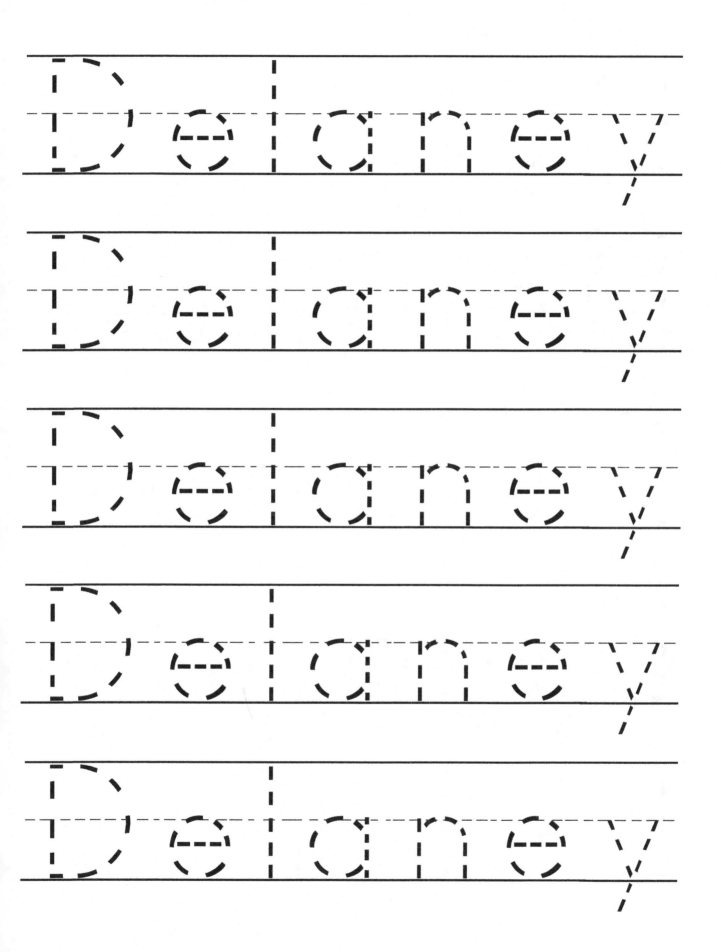

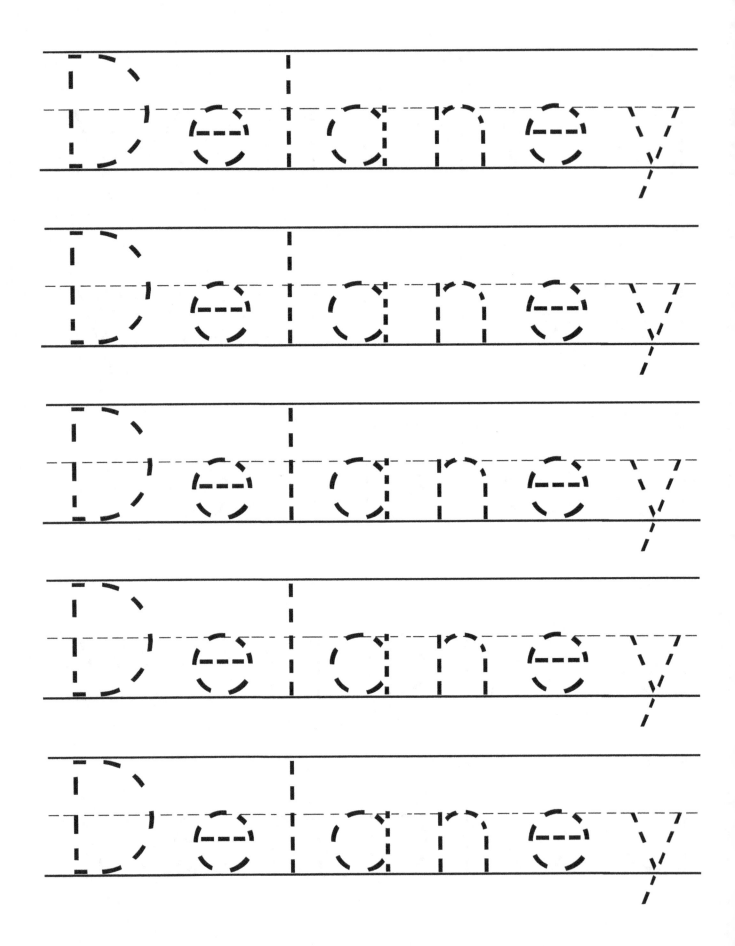

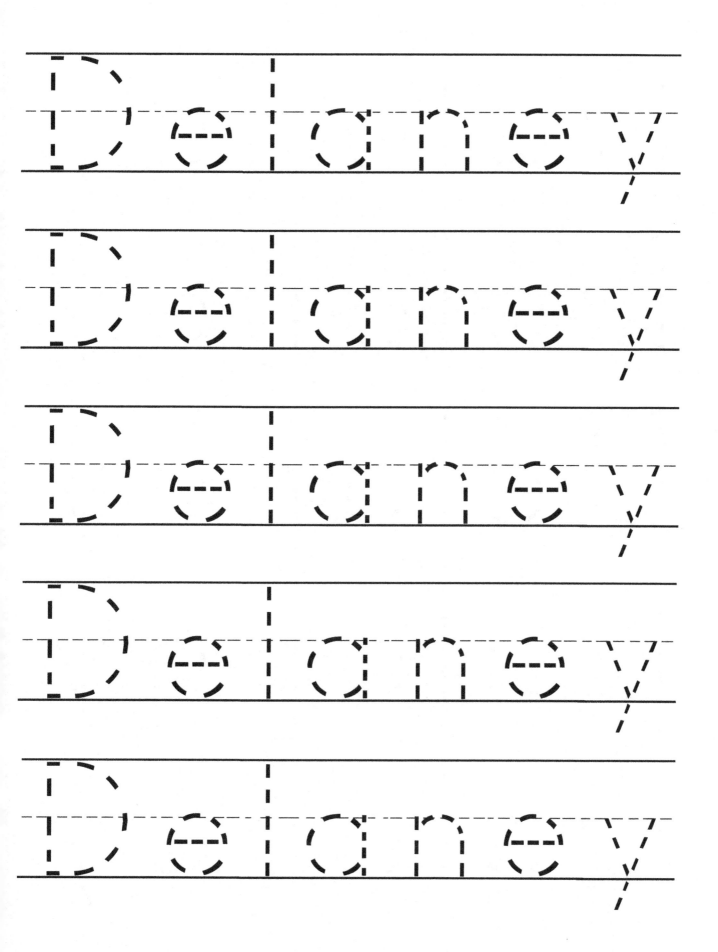

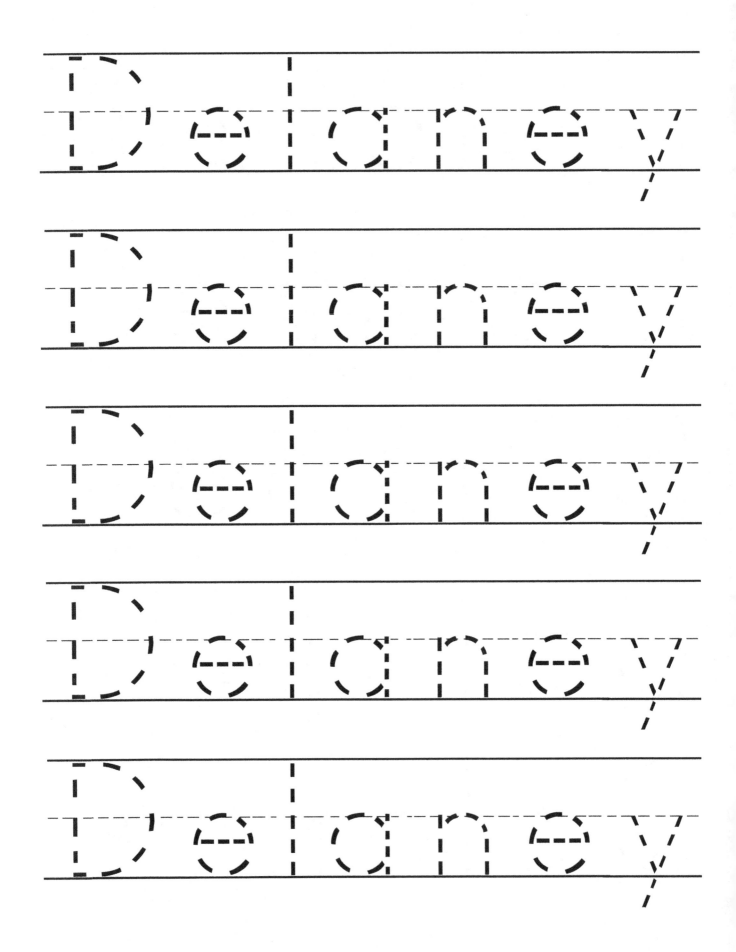

Delaney

Delaney

Delaney

Delaney

Delaney

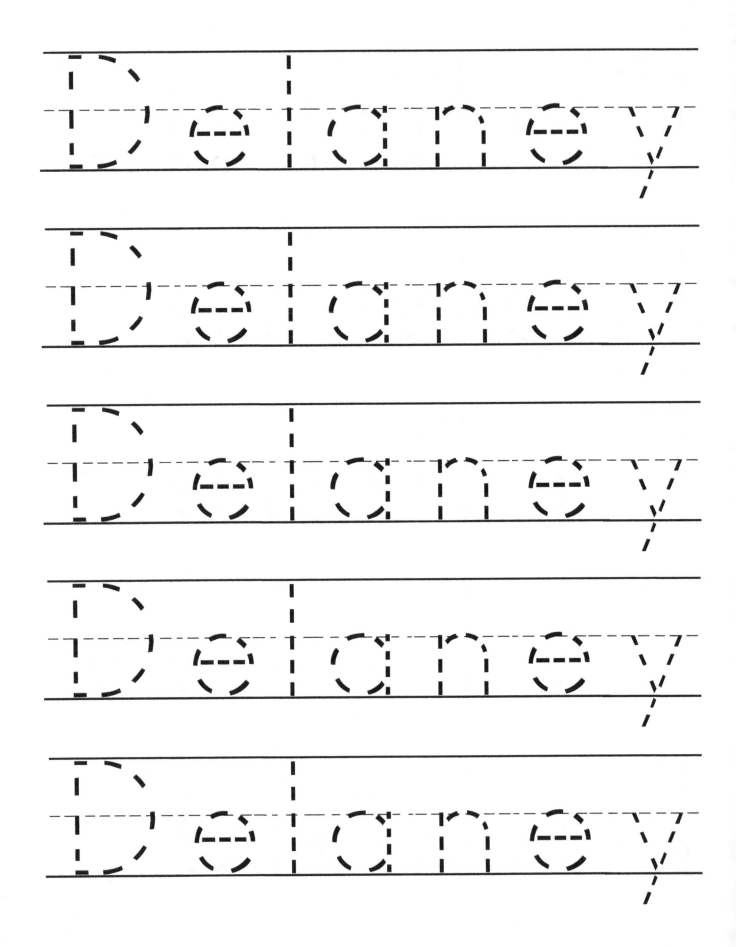

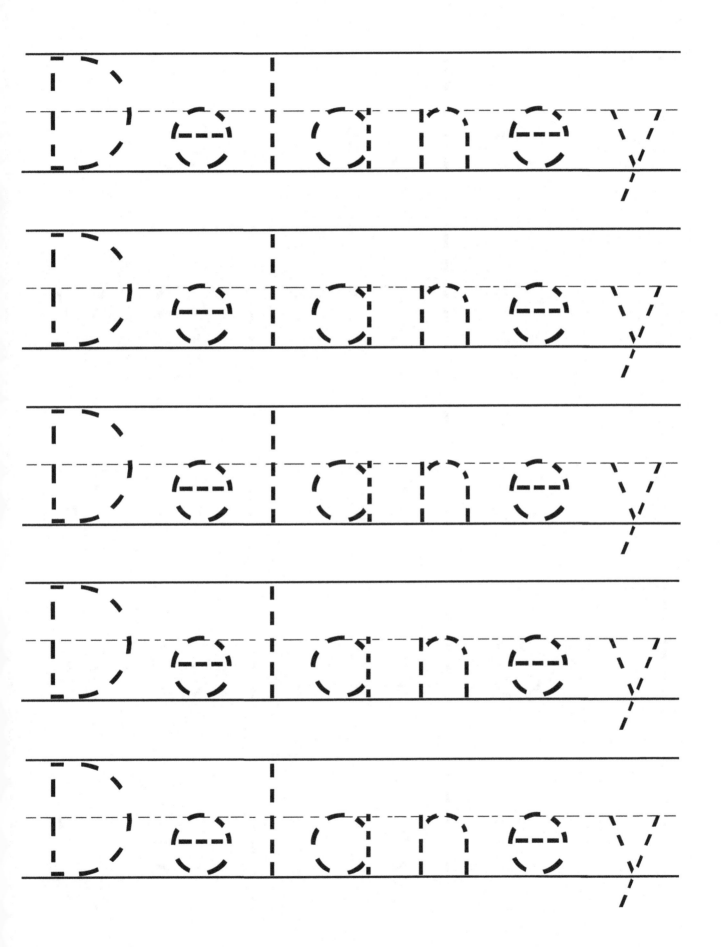

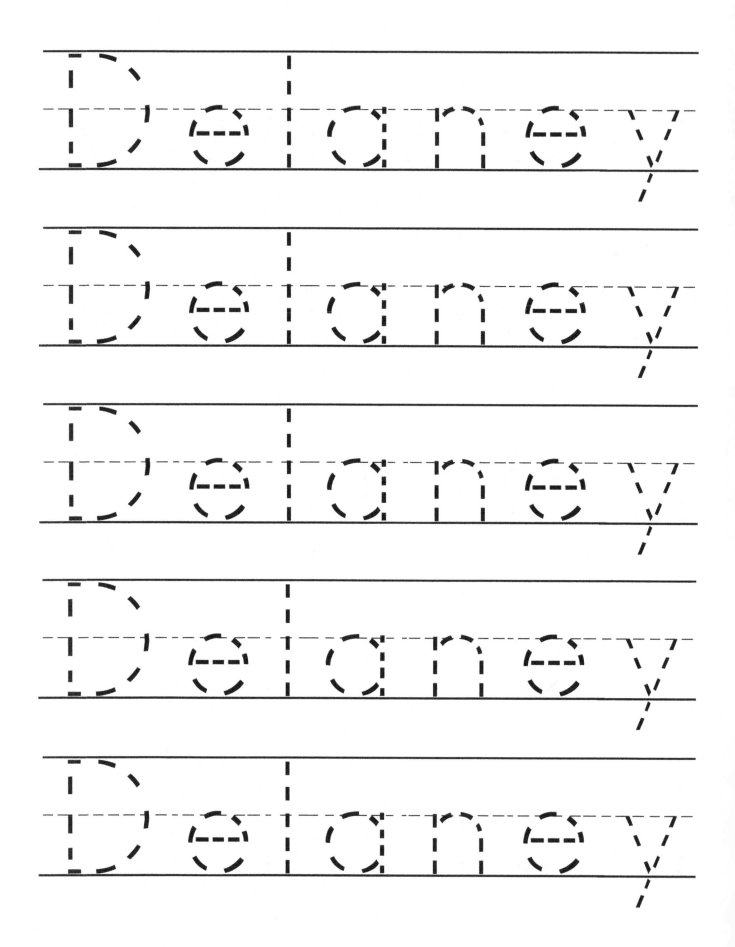

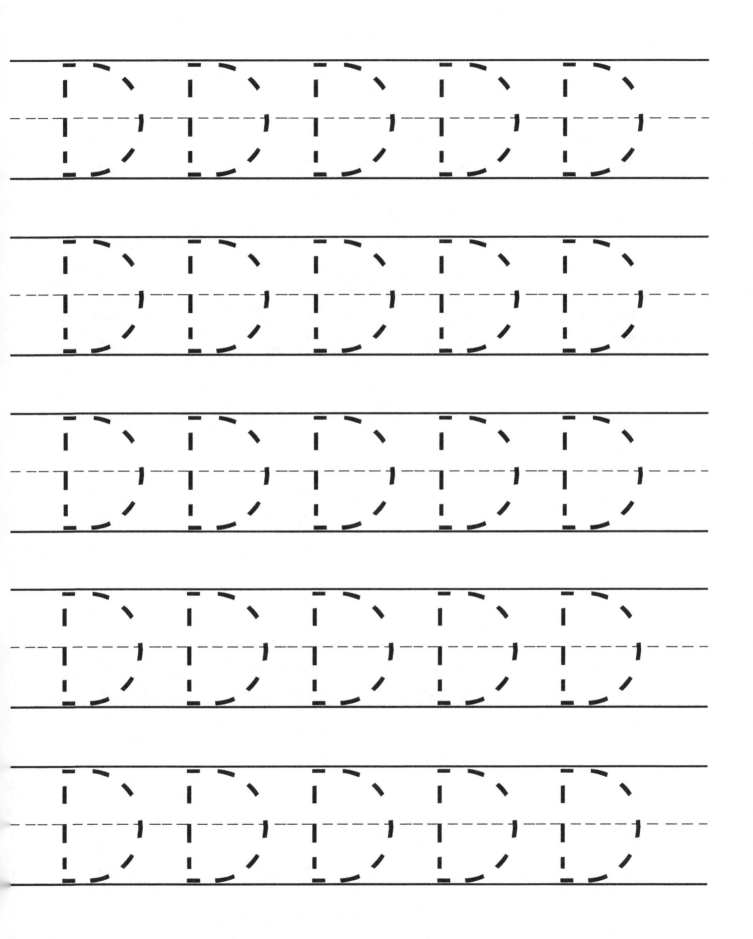

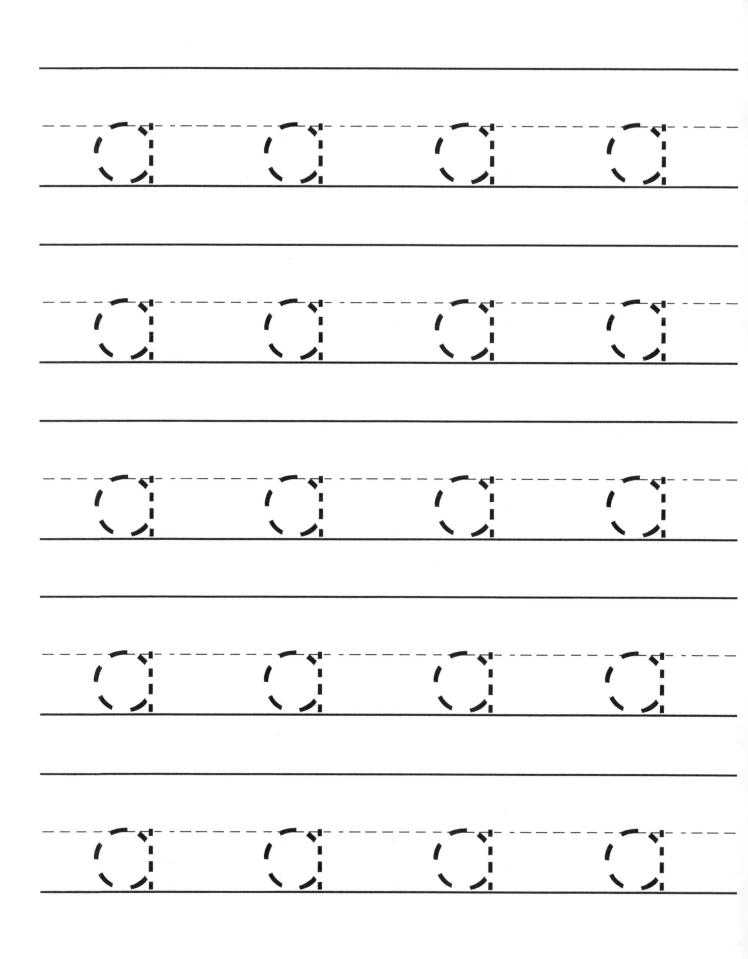

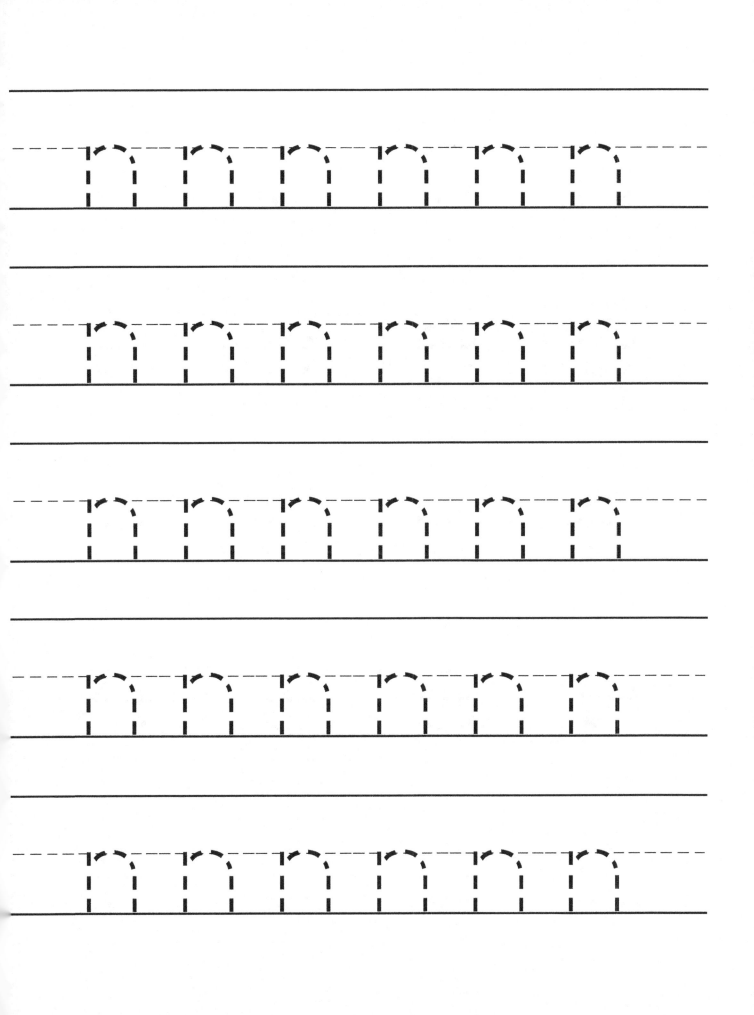

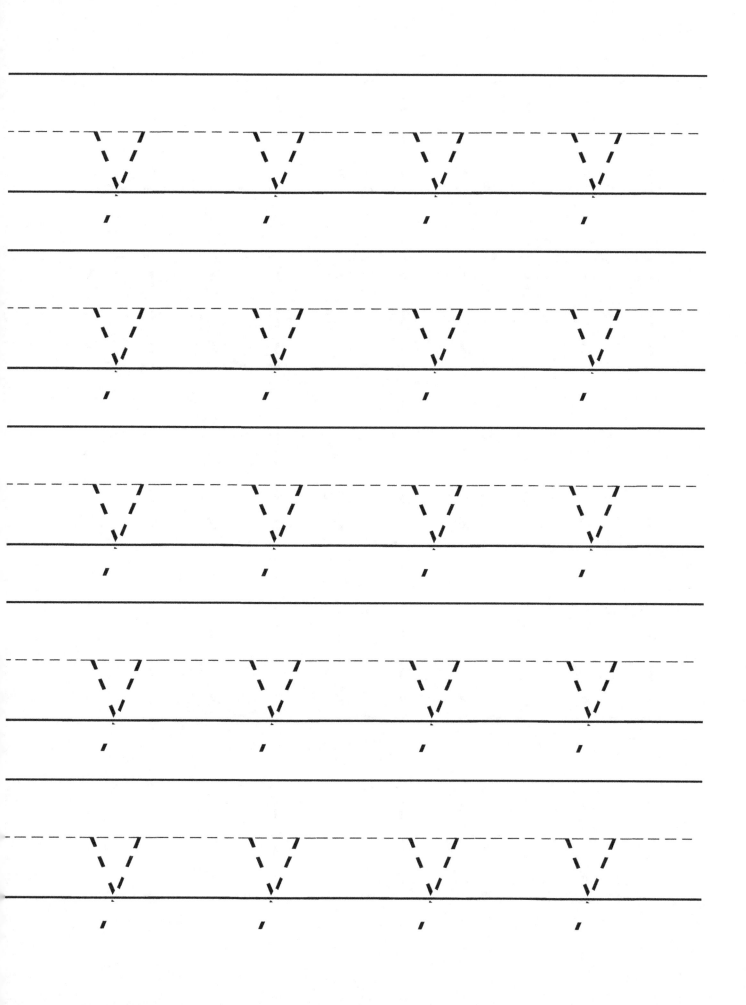

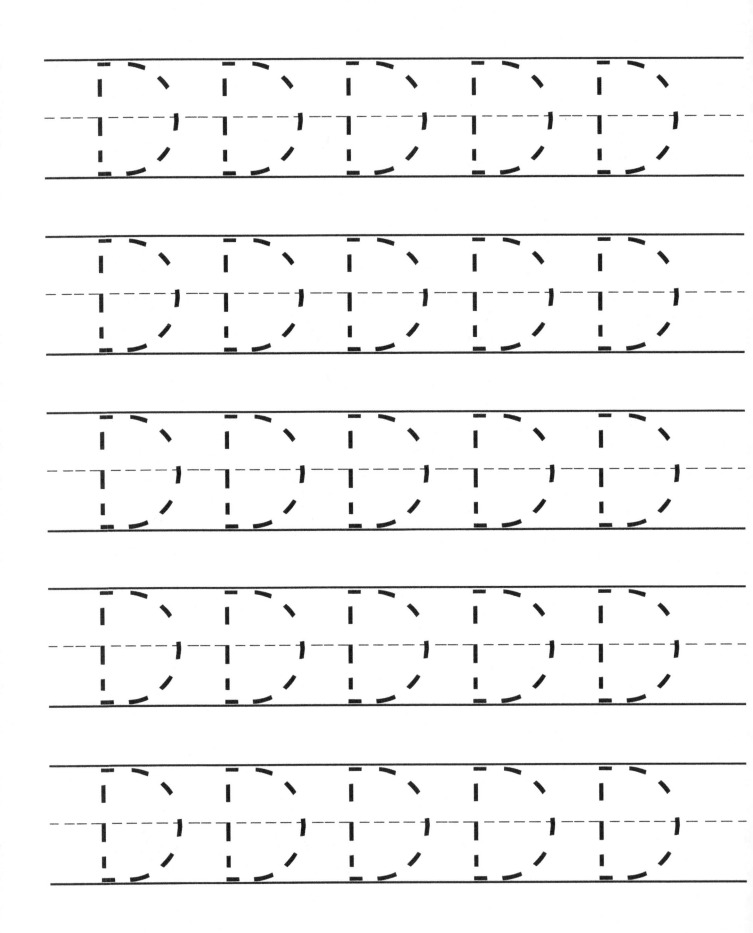

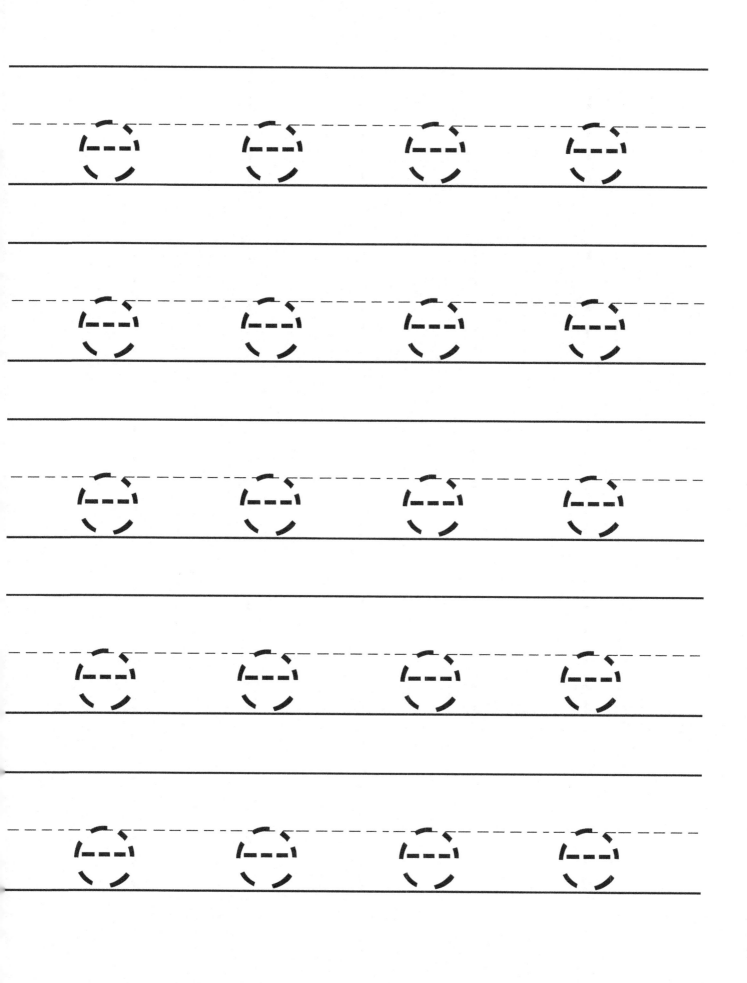

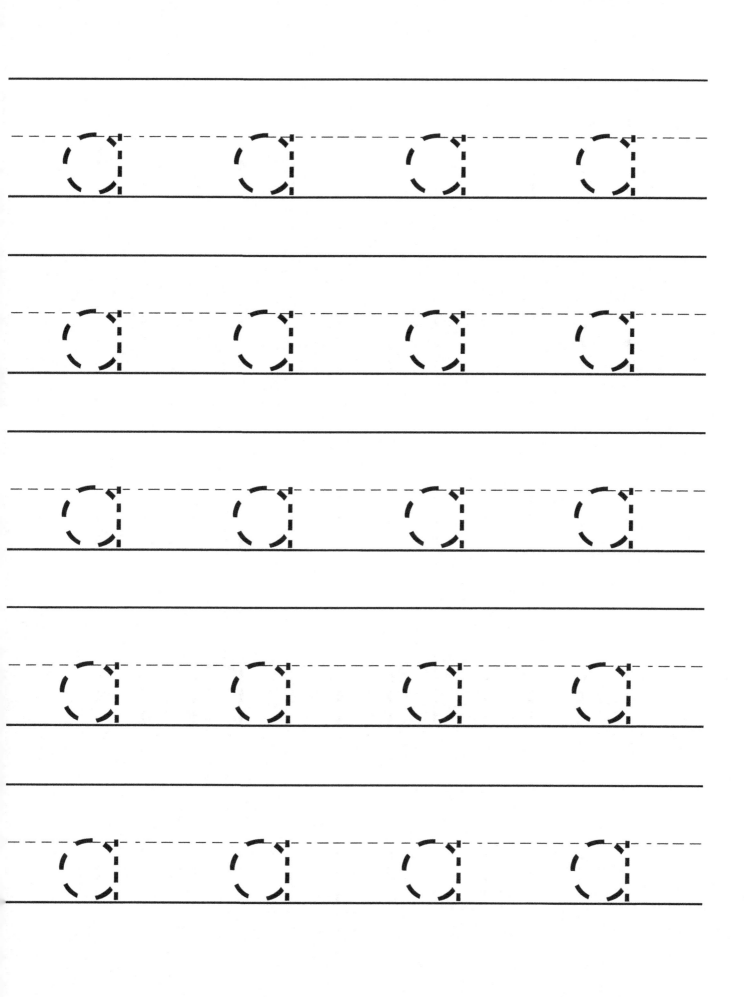

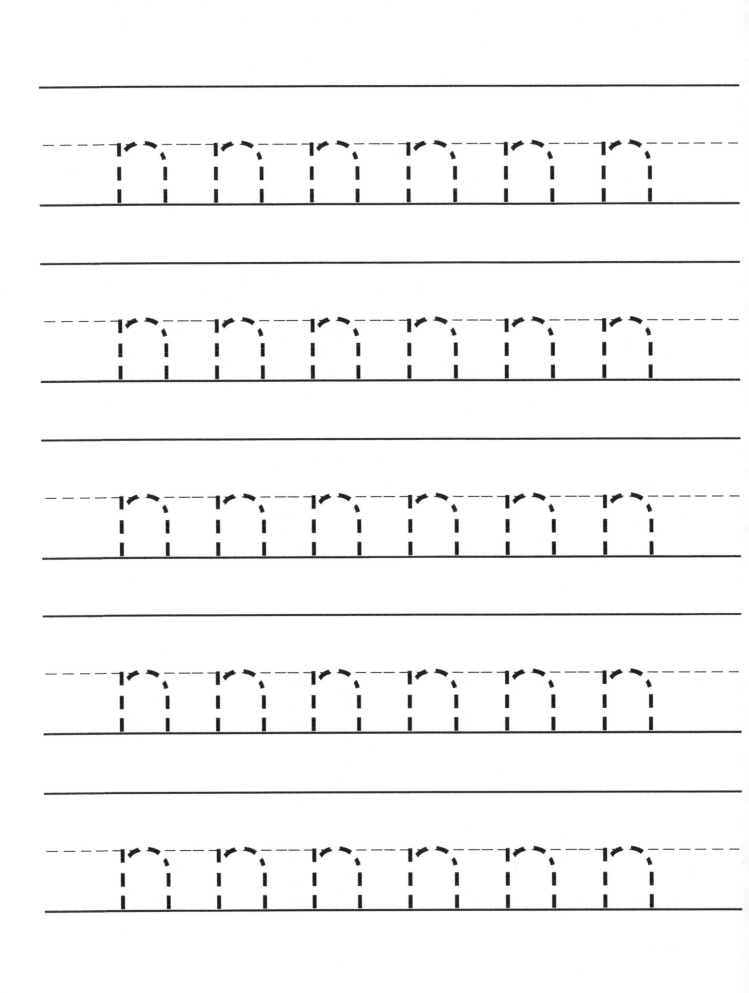

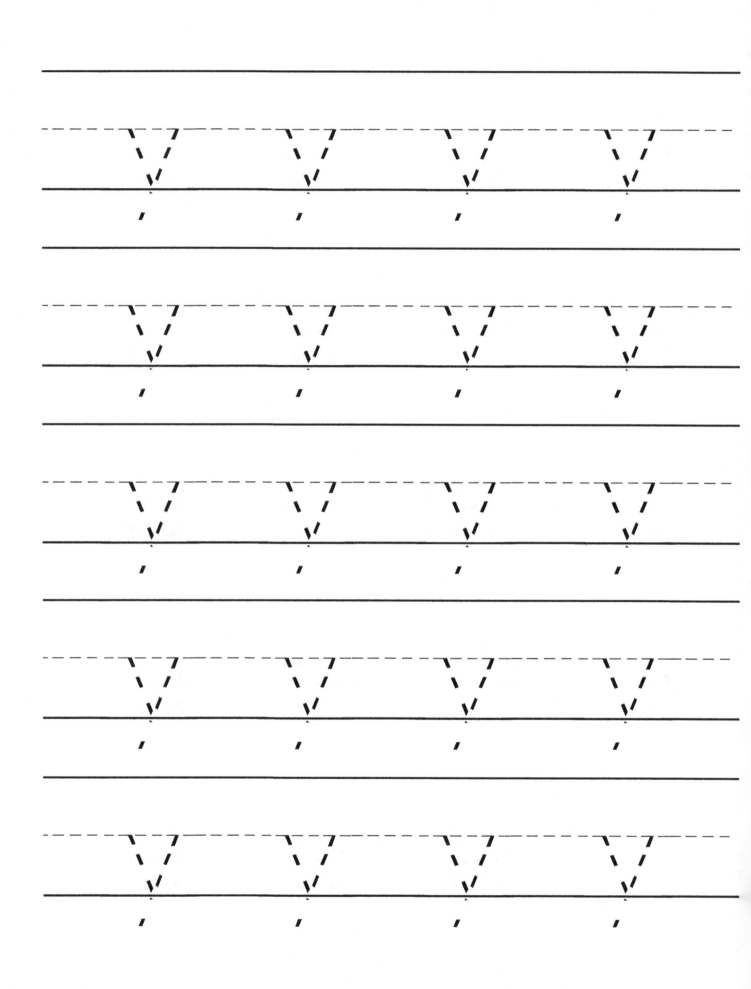

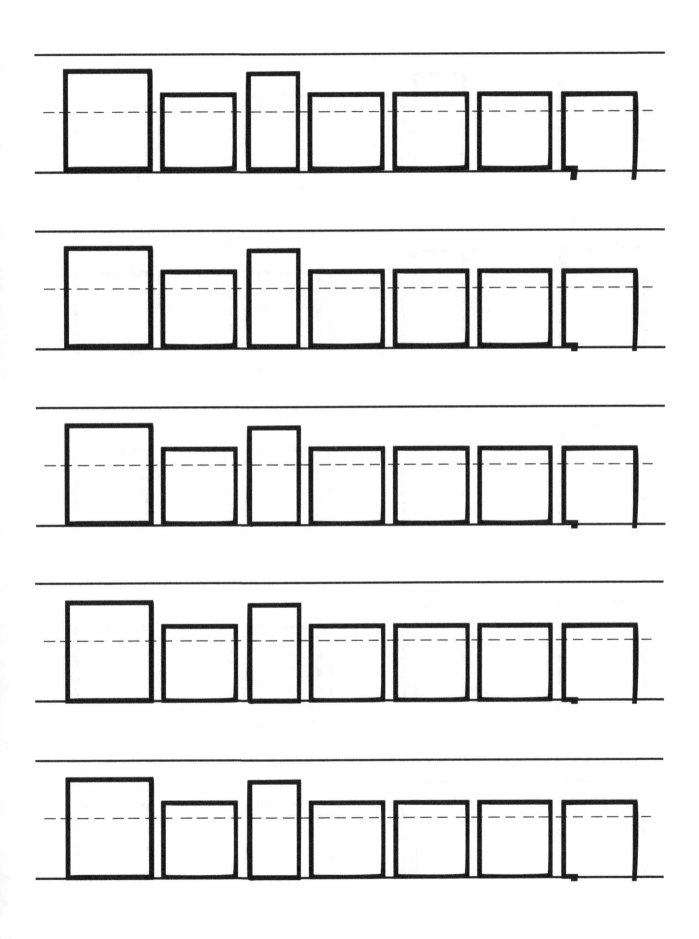

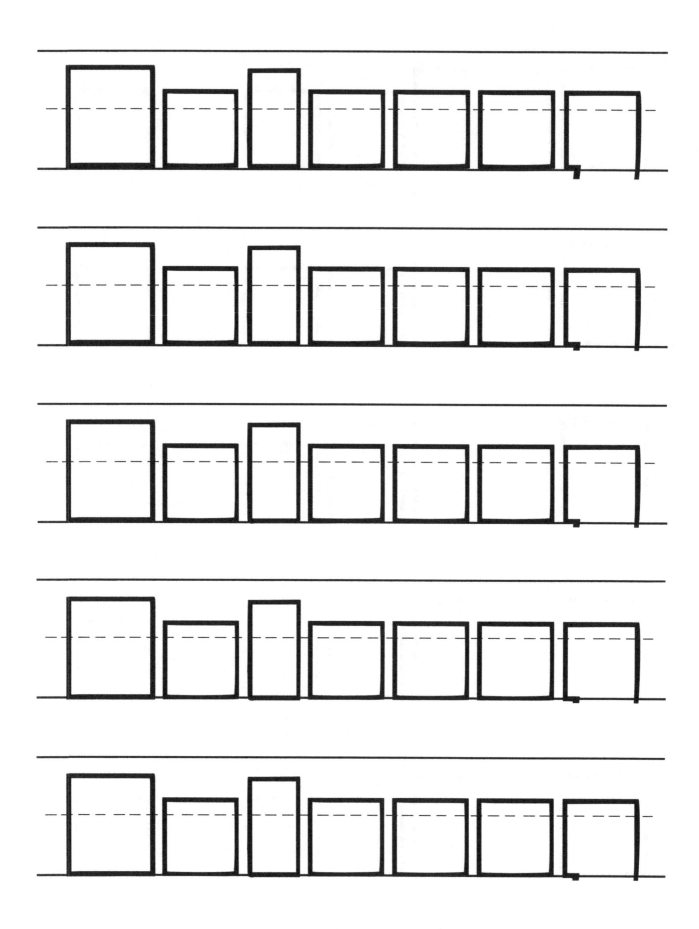

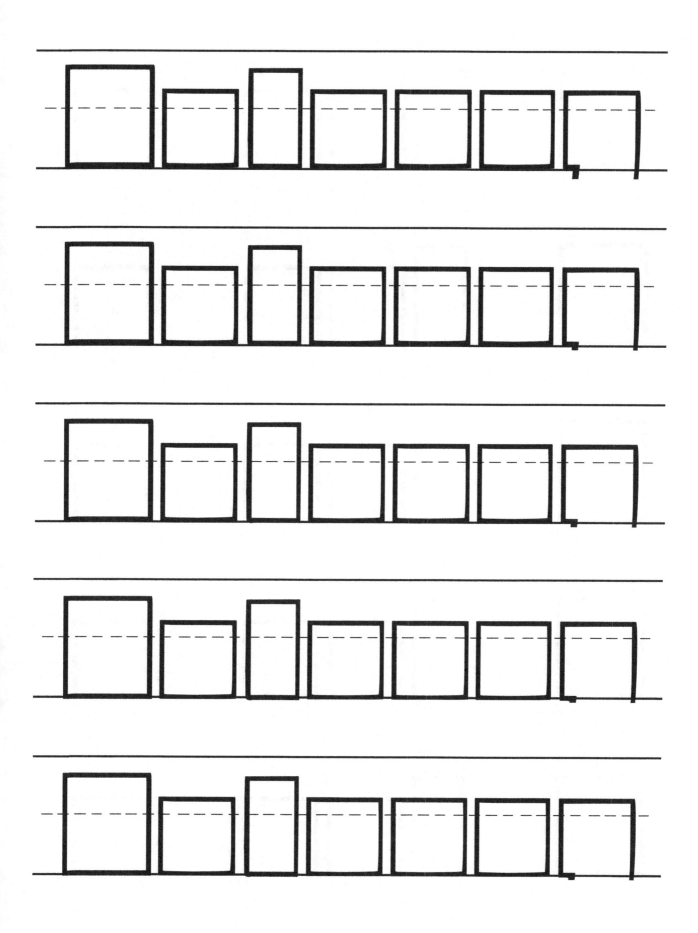

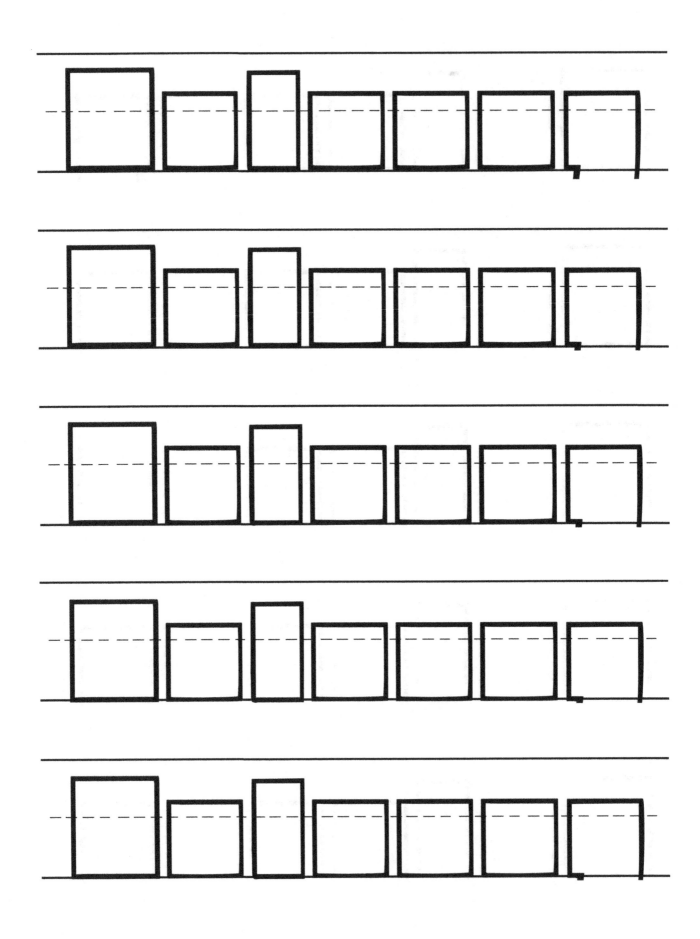

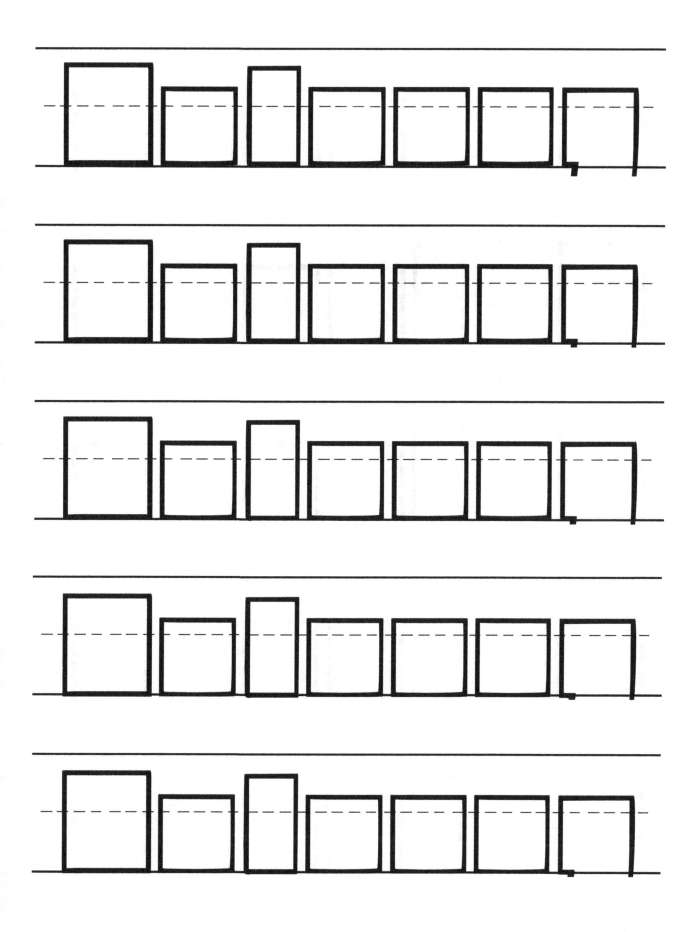

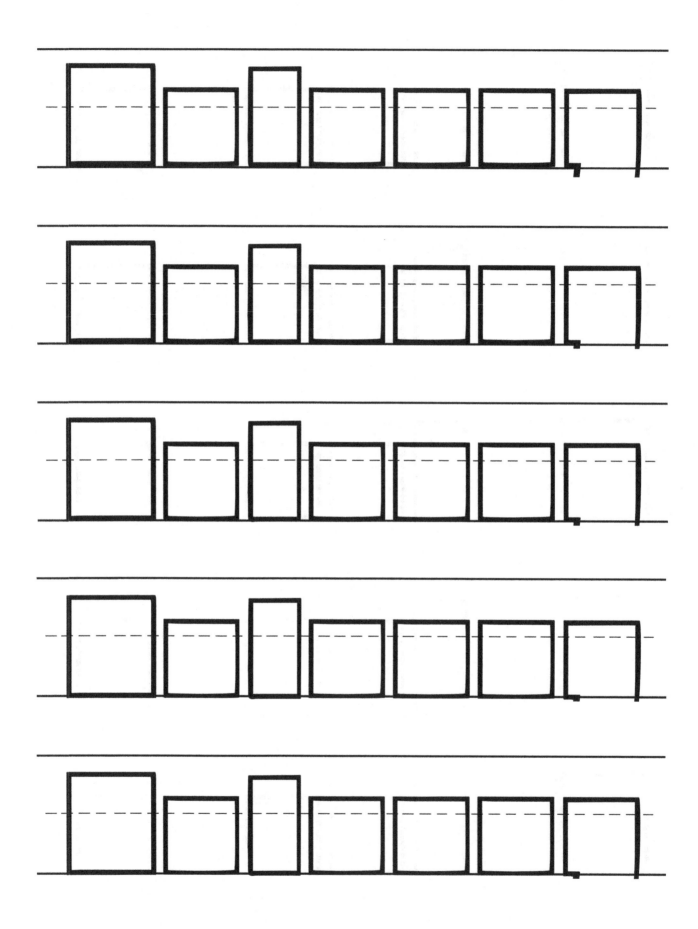

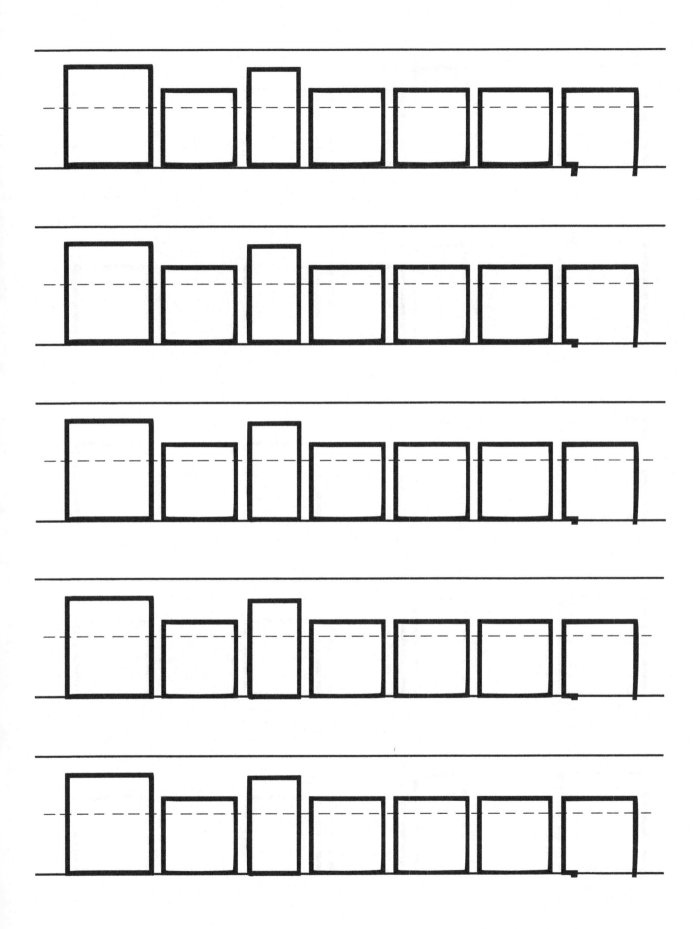

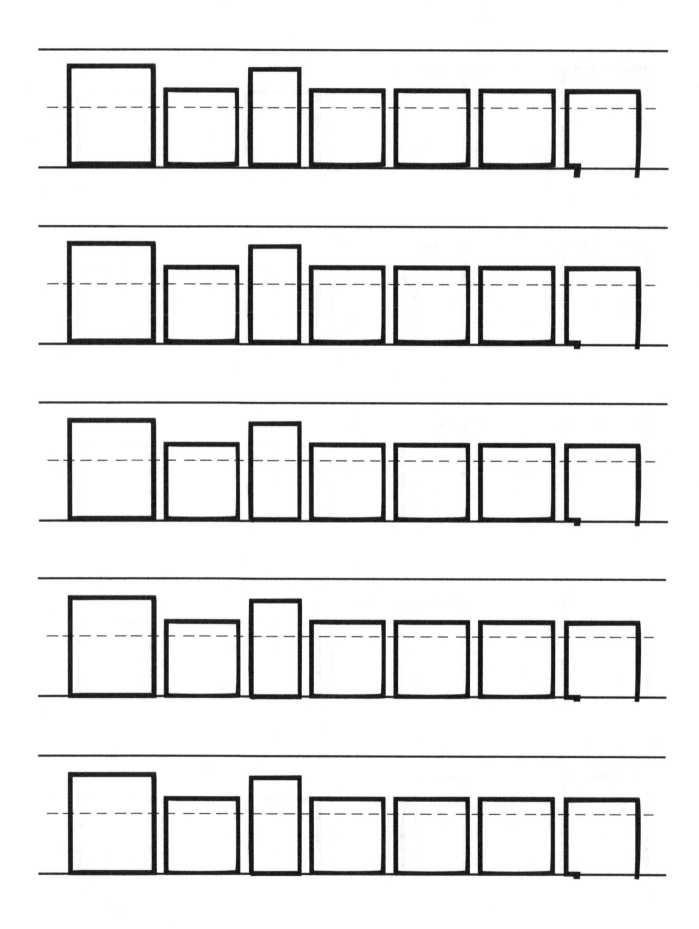

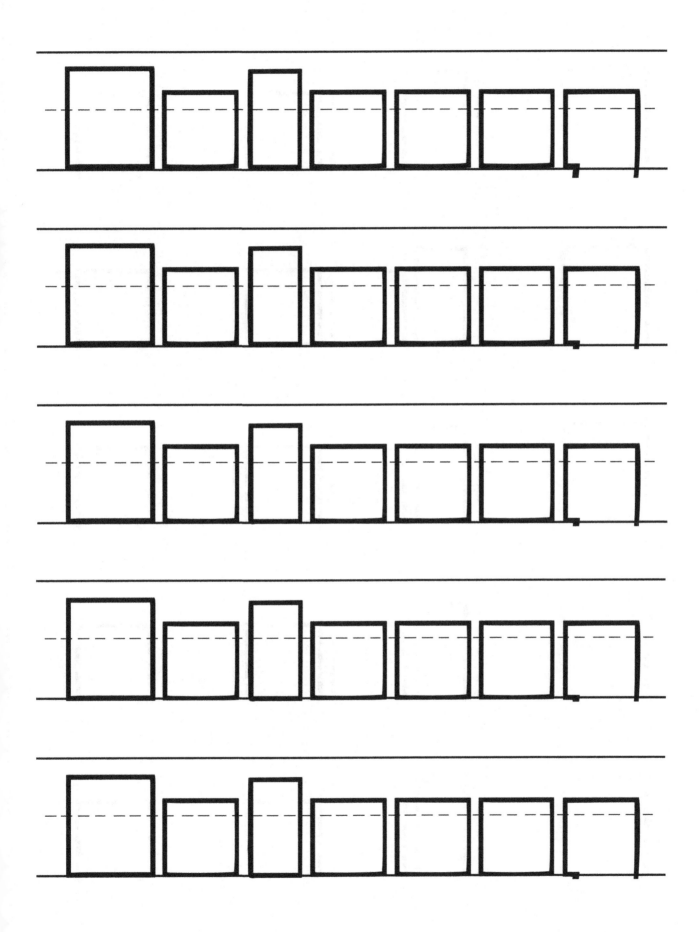

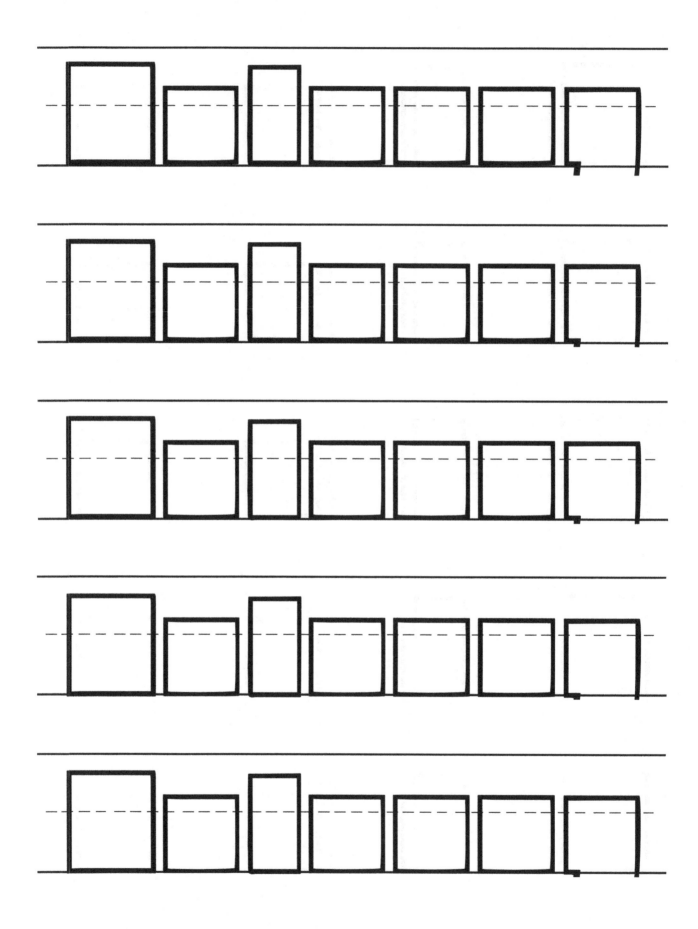

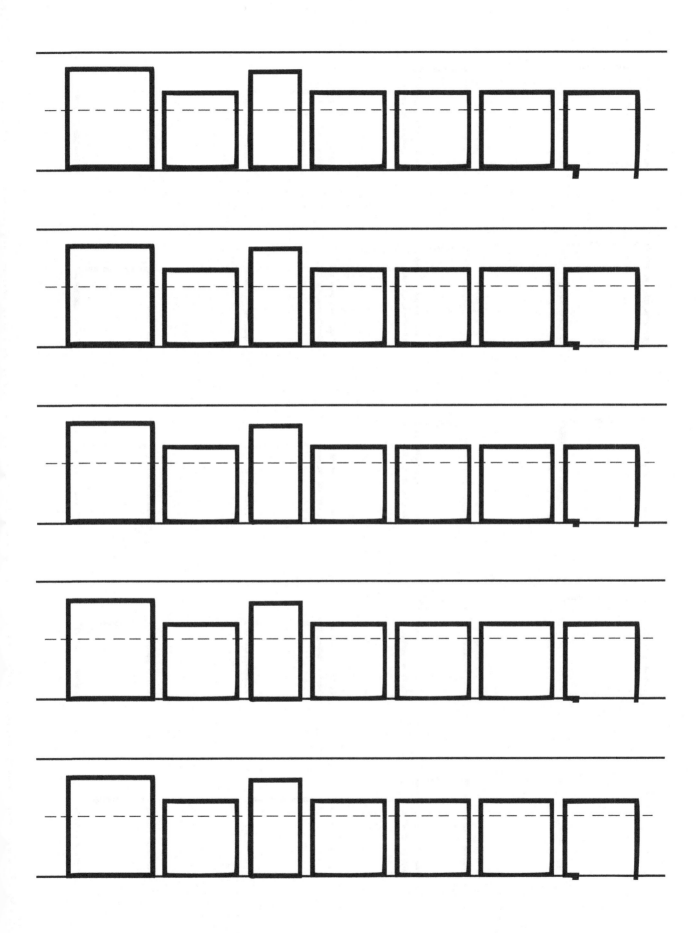

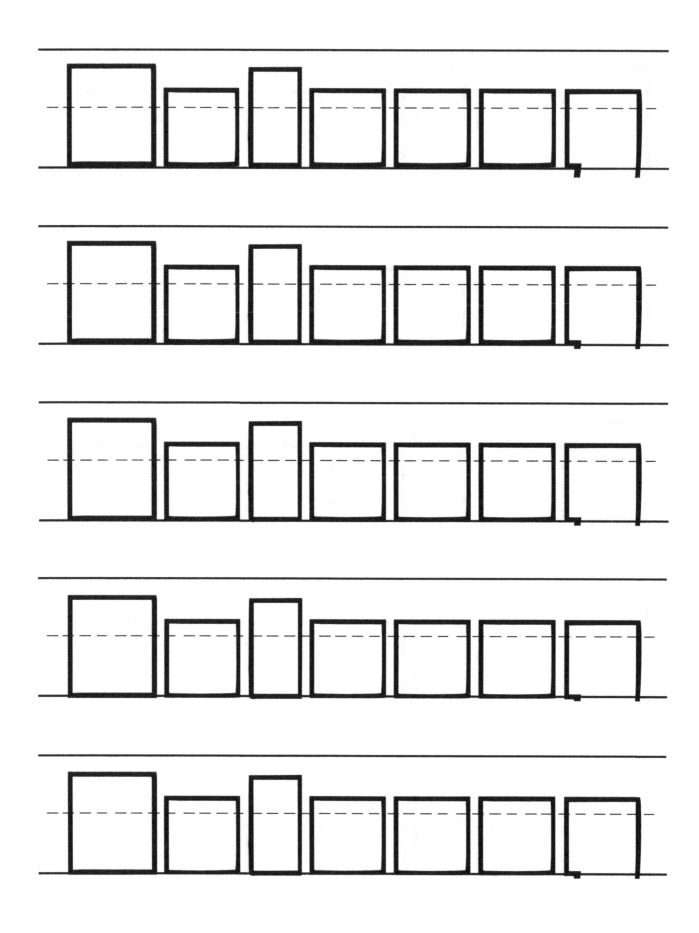

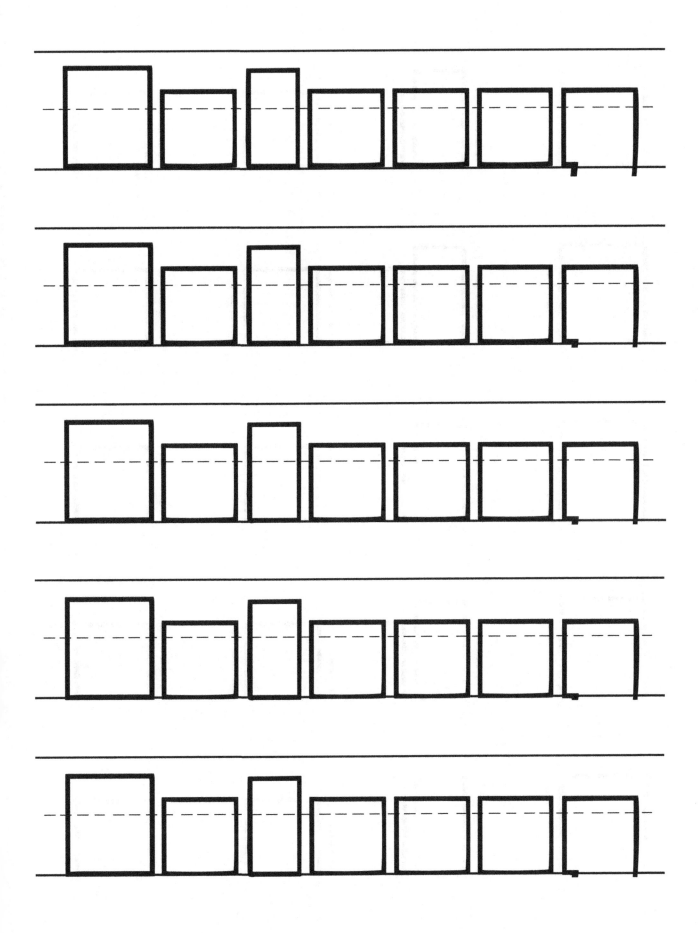

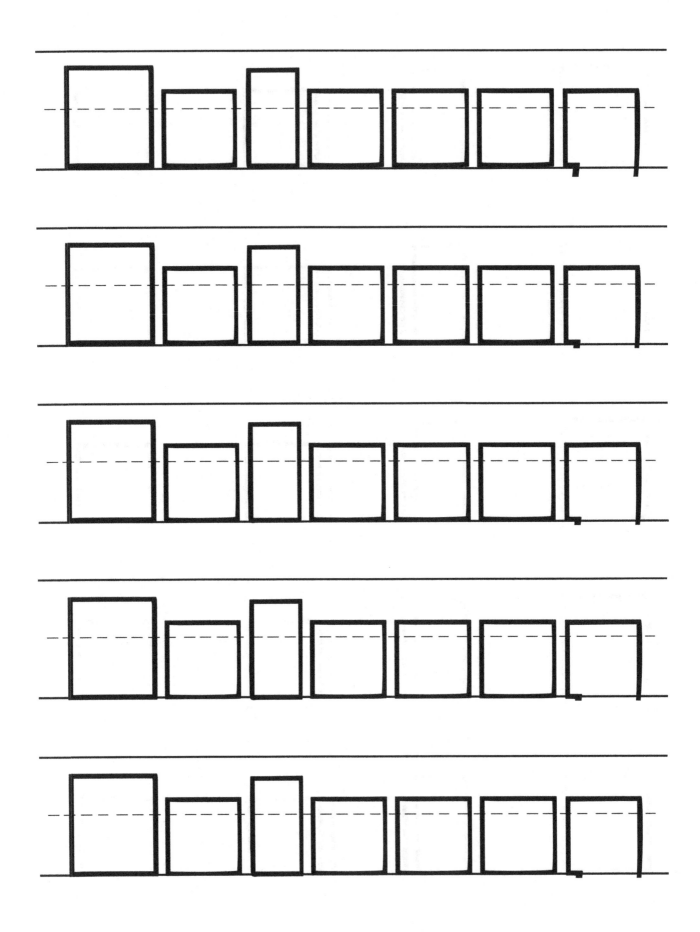

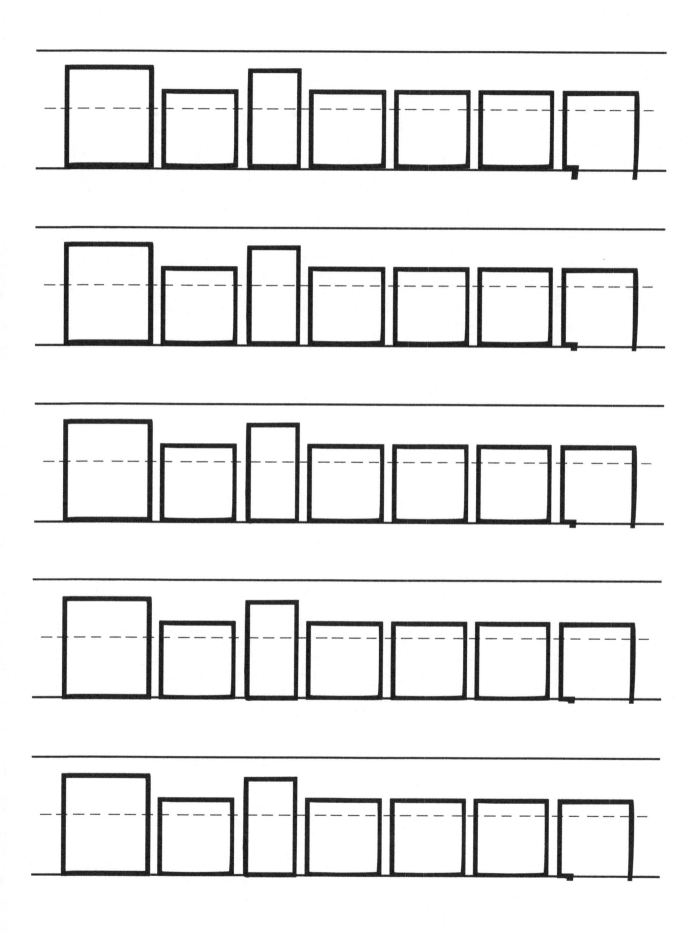

Made in United States
Orlando, FL
27 June 2025

62362796R00057